Remember What You Read
How to Memorize a Book

by

Jim Wiltens

Text and Illustrations by Jim Wiltens

Deer Crossing Press
Redwood City, California

Back cover author photo: Susan Jones

Library of Congress Control Number: 2015942858

$12.00 Pbk

ISBN: 978-0-938525-12-7

Deer Crossing Press
690 Emerald Hill Rd.
Redwood City, CA 94061

Books by Jim Wiltens

Individual Tactics in Waterpolo

Edible and Poisonous Plants of Northern California

No More Nagging, Nit-picking and Nudging: A Guide to Motivating, Inspiring, and Influencing Kids Aged 10–18

Goal Express! The Five Secrets of Goal-Setting Success

Memory Smart: Nine Memory Skills Every Grade Schooler Needs

Camels, Skulls, and Cobras: A Wild Ride Across India

Remember What You Read: How to Memorize a Book

Contents

Introduction

"Concentrate," said the teacher. How many times did you hear this phrase when you were in school? The assumption—if you concentrate, you will remember the material. But there's a glitch. Were you taught how to concentrate? Delving into strategies used by people with super memories, I found that they have a different way of focusing. In *Remember What You Read,* you will discover a powerful way to retain information. The benefits go beyond being able to hold onto what you read.

Benefits of Memorizing a Book

- Your comprehension will increase dramatically. The techniques you are going to learn will teach you how to use pictorial representations for conceptual ideas. To explain the pictures and what they represent, you have to understand what you read. This system transforms you from a passive reader to an active participant.

- Take advantage of the neuro-protective benefits of exercising your brain. Research supports the idea that vigorous mental stimulation is good for the brain. It may help prevent or delay memory loss, dementia, and Alzheimer's.[1, 2, 3, 4] This has resulted in the growth of an Internet industry based on brain games. Memory researchers suggest that these games make you better at playing the game, but no better at practical cognitive tasks.[5] Memorizing a book provides both brain stimulation and a real-world skill.

- Your self-esteem is enhanced. We *are* our memories. Ask any early-stage Alzheimer's patient how devastated he is by the loss of memories. Imagine the opposite: how would you feel if you could improve your memory by 10% or more? Power increases when you are confident. If you have memorized a book, you will be confident about the information from that source.

- You become more creative. Leonardo DaVinci believed that a good memory is necessary to have all the elements readily accessible for the creativity process.[6] There is an "imaginative" aspect connected to memorizing a book that employs visualization and original thought.

1

How to Memorize a Book

Nick frowned. He was doubtful. What he was attempting seemed extremely difficult. He had seen other candidates succeed, but could *he* do it? Nick was enrolled in a leadership training program.[7] A prerequisite for graduation is demonstrating the ability to memorize a book. The rationale for including memory training in the course is to help leadership candidates retain information they study. As memory expert Harry Lorayne says, "There is no learning without memory." The book chosen for this year's program was *Influence: The psychology of persuasion*. It is over 250 pages long. Nick sat next to an evaluator. The evaluator's job is to page through the text as the candidate begins their recitation. The evaluator is not checking for verbatim memory but rather a practical demonstration of recall. Nick would begin at the first chapter, list the main point, and then follow it with an explanation and supporting examples used in the book. He would use his own words to demonstrate full comprehension of the material. Nick started, "The first chapter is titled 'The Weapons of Influence' and starts with the story of a jewelry store owner who ... ." Chapter by chapter, example by example, he worked his way through the text. Sometime later the evaluator came to the last page, closed the cover, and gave Nick a thumbs up. Nick smiled, he had memorized his first book. It was a remarkable performance. Even more remarkable—this genius skill can be performed by many people. Nick had used a mnemonic technique (method for improving memory) that has been taught to diverse audiences including ten-year-old elementary school students, Stanford University staff, and Google employees. *Remember What You Read* will prepare you to memorize your first book. Once you have learned the technique, you can apply it to any book.

In one of my earlier books, *Memory Smart,* there is a chapter on how to memorize *any* book.[8] The process is fully explained, but the practice section is short. In workshops, I find that attendees have a better grasp of the technique when, rather than a short practice section, they actually memorize an entire book. So I worked out the mnemonic details necessary to memorize three mainstream books:

- *Influence: The psychology of persuasion,* Robert B. Cialdini
- *Cracking Creativity: The secrets of creative genius,* Michael Michalko
- *Made to Stick: Why some ideas survive and others die,* Chip Heath and Dan Heath

You are about to learn how to memorize one or all of these books. Each of these books contains powerful behavioral principles which, if remembered and practiced, can increase your power. These techniques can also be used to memorize only a portion of a book or an outline of a book and several supporting examples for each main point.

Substitution: Replace Words with Pictures

To memorize a book, wordy-ideas are converted into images. Think of these images as visual metaphors. The reason for this conversion is that images are easier to remember than words. [9, 10, 11, 12] Researchers call this image over word preference the "picture superiority effect."

In mnemonics, the replacement of an image for a word is known as a substitution technique. For example, a substitute image for the first amendment of the U.S. Constitution—freedom of speech, assembly, press, and religion—could be a man speaking (speech) to a large crowd (assembly) while typing (press) and sitting on a cross (religion) (figure 1-1).

1-1 Converting a conceptual idea, in this case the first amendment to the U.S. Constitution, into a visual metaphor. The person speaking represents freedom of speech. The group of people represents freedom of assembly, the keyboard represents freedom of the press, and the cross stands for freedom of religion.

The second amendment—the right to bear arms—might be a bear carrying a rifle (figure 1-2).

1-2 The second amendment to the U.S. Constitution, the right to bear arms, converted into an graphic metaphor of a bear with a gun.

Substitution is a time-tested mnemonic device. Rock stars of ancient Greece, like the poet Simonides, used substitution in the fifth century BC to memorize lengthy poems. In the Middle Ages, the paintings and stained glass windows in cathedrals depicting biblical scenes jogged the memories of churchgoers to contemplate stories from the Bible.[13, 14] Mark Twain used it to deliver speeches without notes.[15] Present day world-class memory athlete Bruce Balmer used substitution to memorize 2000 foreign language words in a single day.[16] It is a versatile mnemonic technique.

To memorize a book, the first step is to convert concepts into images. In *Remember What You Read*, the substitute image construction has been done for you. For example, in the book *Influence*, the first chapter starts with the story of a shop owner who was having trouble selling a collection of turquoise jewelry. The jewelry was good quality, priced right, but it wasn't selling during her busiest season. She tried a variety of selling tactics.

Nothing worked. Finally, in exasperation, she left a note for her sales staff. "Everything in this display case, price x ½." When she returned to her shop she was surprised to find that the jewelry had sold like hot cakes. Even more surprising—it had sold for twice the original price. Her assistant had misread the note. Rather than cut the price in half, she had doubled it. The owner was at a loss to explain why doubling the price had resulted in selling out the item. The author, a psychologist, goes on to explain the mystery.

To apply substitution to this story, imagine a bin filled with turquoise jewelry. A sign in the bin shows $1 crossed out and $2 next to it (figure 1-3).

1-3. The turquoise jewelry story from the book *Influence*, converted into a graphic substitution.

This image is sufficient for most people to recall the details of the story.

Let's take two more concepts from *Influence* and convert them into substitute images. These additional images will be used in a moment to illustrate a second mnemonic technique that is necessary to memorize a book.

In the book *Influence*, a description of animal behavior follows the turquoise jewelry story. The example given is that of a female turkey. Maternal turkeys are programmed to nurture their brood based on hearing the cheep-cheep sound of young turkey chicks. The sound is an important trigger for chick survival. Without this sound, turkey mothers will ignore or kill a chick. A dramatic illustration of how the cheep-cheep sound affects turkeys can be seen in the response of a mother turkey to her mortal enemy—the polecat. Even a stuffed polecat, when drawn by a string towards a mother turkey, will elicit a vicious pecking-clawing-wing-beating attack. But when researchers installed a tape recorder that played the cheep-cheep sound in the stuffed polecat, momma turkey took the polecat under her wing. Turn off the recorder and the polecat was attacked by the turkey. The substitute image could be a turkey next to a polecat (figure 1-4).

1-4 The turkey-polecat story from the book *Influence* converted into a graphic substitution.

The next idea covered in *Influence* is what animal behaviorists call a fixed action pattern. The robotic reaction of the turkey to *cheep-cheep* is a fixed action pattern. It is as if a tape recorder button is pressed and click-whirr a consistent behavior runs like a programmed tape. What is interesting is that only a single trigger is necessary to elicit the behavior. For instance, a male robin defends its territory by attacking other male robins. The trigger in this case is red feathers. A robin will attack a clump of red feathers vigorously, yet it will ignore a perfectly stuffed replica of a robin—without red breast feathers. These fixed action patterns are also found in humans. If someone knows the trigger, they can dupe a human as readily as the researchers duped the turkey and the robin.

The image we will use to represent the fixed action pattern is a tape recorder with a robin wearing boxing gloves pummeling a clump of red feathers (figure 1-5).

1-5 The fixed action pattern and red robin story from the book *Influence* converted into a graphic substitution.

Chaining: Making a Memory Charm Bracelet

Now we have converted three stories from *Influence* into substitute images: the turquoise jewelry bin, a turkey sheltering a polecat, and a pugilistic robin on a tape recorder. As the number of images increases, it gets harder to keep track of them. This is where the second mnemonic technique comes into play—chaining. Chaining is the mnemonic version of a memory charm bracelet. Like a charm bracelet, each link in a mnemonic chain has a piece of information attached to it. To retrieve images, you work your way along the chain.

When you tell the story of *Goldilocks and the Three Bears,* you are chaining. You begin with Goldilocks entering the house and discovering the porridge in the kitchen, followed by the chairs fiasco in the living room, which leads to the beds in the bedroom and the bears' discovery of a fairy tale juvenile delinquent in their home. Each act in this mini-play prompts your memory to the next scene.

If we apply chaining to the substitute images we have constructed for *Influence*, it might go like this. The jewelry bin launches a turquoise necklace into the air. The necklace lands on the turkey's neck (figure 1-6).

1-6 Two graphic substitutions based on stories from the book *Influence* are chained together. Imagine a piece of turquoise jewelry flying out of the jewelry bin and landing around the turkey's neck.

The polecat standing next to the turkey is startled by its movement and backs into a tape recorder and a clump of red feathers. This prompts a robin to hop on the recorder, activating the tape, click-whirr, and start punching the feathers (figure 1-7).

1-7 Two graphic substitutions based on stories from the book *Influence* are chained together. A startled polecat backs into a tape recorder occupied by a robin attacking a bundle of red feathers.

Each image is linked by an action that leads to the next image in the chain. This is how the students mentioned at the beginning of this chapter memorized *Influence*. Major ideas in the book were converted into 72 graphic substitutions. The images were then sequentially chained together with actions. By working their way along this mini-movie script of chained illustrations, the students were able to recall the information represented by each substitution graphic.

Visualize It!

Chaining images requires that you visualize the images and the action that connects them. Memory experts agree that seeing mental images in your mind's eye is a must. An example of creating a mental image would be to imagine the capital letters D and J. Rotate the "D" 90 degrees counter clockwise in your mind. Now put the J underneath it. What graphic image do you see?[17]

When a beginner practices visualization, you will occasionally see him silently moving his lips. This could indicate that the student is not visualizing. He is saying the words in his mind rather than seeing images. This accounts for the unconscious lip movement. He is creating virtual sounds, not virtual images. Talking through the chain is not as memory effective as seeing it. If you want to remember it, you must see it in your mind. A general rule is to hold the image in your mind for a minimum of 10 seconds (see Chapter 5 for more details on this 10-second rule).

Three Steps to Memorize a Book

1. Look at the first image in the chain for the book you are memorizing. Make a mental snapshot. Close your eyes and visualize this image for a minimum of 10 uninterrupted seconds.
2. Look at the next picture. Again, make a snapshot and hold it on your mental screen for 10 seconds.
3. Now chain the first image to the second with some action. Make the interaction between the two scenes dynamic, watch it like a movie for 10 seconds. Repeat for the next image in the chain.

I recommend chaining six pictures. Then start reading the book they apply to. As you read, there will be little *aha* moments when you recognize how the substitute image applies to the text. Each image is a tiny riddle. This is good for goading your brain to pay attention.

When you reach a point in the book where your memorized images run out, memorize another six pictures and resume reading. When you have the entire sequence of images committed to memory, go back through them to see if you have full comprehension of what each visual metaphor represents in the book.

You are not memorizing the book word for word. Instead you are building a full outline with supporting examples. Where there were multiple examples of a single topic or idea, I chose the most salient to include in the memory chain.

Which Book Are You Going to Memorize?

You now have sufficient information to start memorizing one of the three books mentioned at the beginning of this chapter. If you want more background on why the technique works, check out Chapter 5. Chapter 5 also contains tips to make your memory more effective in general.

Now it is time to obtain a copy of the book you want to memorize. To help you decide which book to start with, you will find short summaries, along with the graphic substitutions for that book, in each of the following chapters. The specific edition is included here to ensure a match between the book you select and the page numbers beneath each graphic substitution:

- Chapter 2: *Influence: The psychology of persuasion*. Robert B. Cialdini. 2007 edition (ISBN 978-0-06-124189-5) published by Harper Collins Publishers.
- Chapter 3: *Cracking Creativity: The secrets of creative genius*. Michael Michalko. 1998 edition (ISBN 0-89815-913-X) published by Ten Speed Press.
- Chapter 4: *Made to Stick: Why some ideas survive and others die*. Chip Heath and Dan Heath. 2007 edition (ISBN 978-1-4000-6428-1) published by Random House.

All the books were picked based on their usefulness. They contain universal skills. Each book is a potential life changer—if you can remember what you have read.

2

Mnemonic Graphics for the Book *Influence*

In the book *Influence: The psychology of persuasion*, Robert Cialdini shows how masters of persuasion work their trade. Some of his research involved going undercover. He worked in advertising, door-to-door sales, fund raising, real estate, car sales and received on-the-job training from real-world influence professionals. As a psychologist, he distilled down the tactics of these influencers into six psychological principles. He shows how the right trigger can get you to say "yes" to purchases, donations, concessions, votes, and assenting without thinking. Awareness of these triggers can help you avoid being unduly influenced. It also shows you how to use these techniques to persuade employees, children, spouses, groups, etc.

Explanation of Graphic Construction

Concepts in the book *Influence* were transformed into 72 metaphorical illustrations—graphic substitutions. Below each illustration is a gray box (figure 2-1). It contains a short description of what the graphic refers to in the book. In addition to these descriptor words, you will occasionally find parentheses around several words. This parenthetical group of words is an explanation of how the substitute image was derived. In this example, the closest sounding wording to "Liking" is a "lying king." There are only a few of these. Most graphics make sense after reading the appropriate section in *Influence*. The page numbers for the specific section of the book referenced by the graphic are listed at the end of the description and are based on the 2007 edition of *Influence* (ISBN 978-0-06-124189-5) published by Harper Collins Publishers.

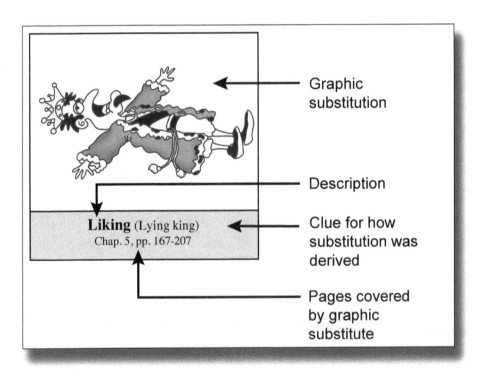

2-1 Explanation of graphic construction.

Weapons of influence
Chap. 1, pp. 1-16

Turquoise sale
pp. 1-2, 5-6

Turkey polecat
pp. 2-4

Click-whirr
p. 3

Can I … because
pp. 4-5

Deadly firefly
p. 8

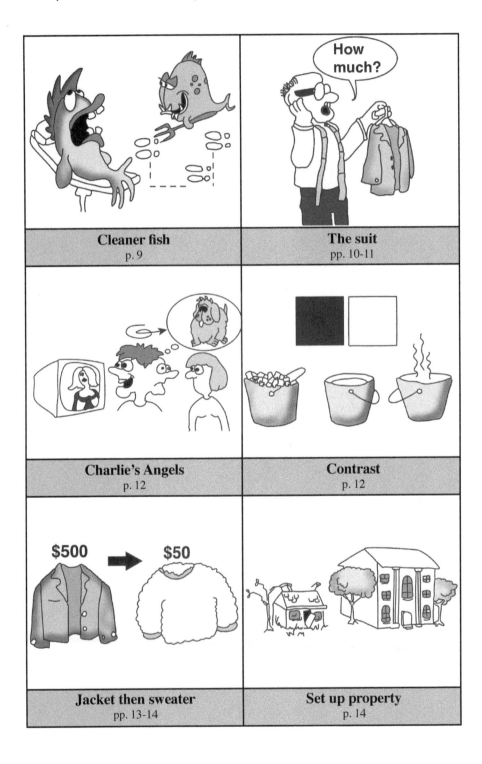

Auto purchase add-ons	Reciprocation (re-sip)
p. 14	Chap. 2, pp. 17-56
Xmas cards	Coke-raffle
p. 17	pp. 20, 34
Krishnas	Amway bug
pp. 22-24, 31-33	pp. 27-28

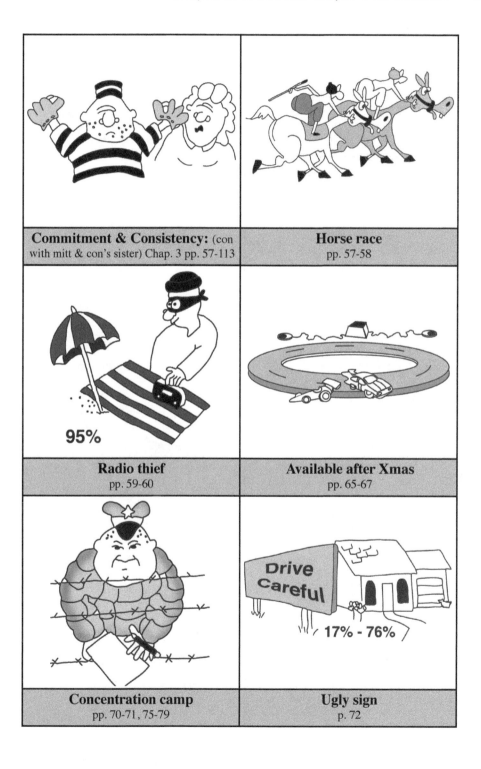

Commitment & Consistency: (con with mitt & con's sister) Chap. 3 pp. 57-113	Horse race pp. 57-58
Radio thief pp. 59-60	Available after Xmas pp. 65-67
Concentration camp pp. 70-71, 75-79	Ugly sign p. 72

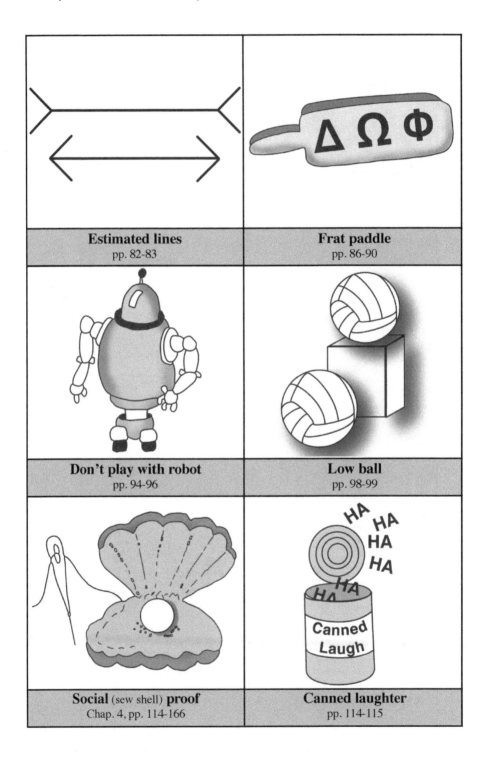

Estimated lines pp. 82-83	**Frat paddle** pp. 86-90
Don't play with robot pp. 94-96	**Low ball** pp. 98-99
Social (sew shell) **proof** Chap. 4, pp. 114-166	**Canned laughter** pp. 114-115

Phobia movie p. 118	Pre-schooler isolation movie p. 119
End of world today pp. 120-128	Genovese killing pp. 129-133
Fire-Fire pp. 134-135	Returned wallet pp. 140-142

Suicide copy cat pp. 145-151	**Jim Jones' poison Kool-aid** pp. 152-156
Opera claquers pp. 158-159	**Turn signals** pp. 162-163
Liking (lying king) Chap. 5, pp. 167-207	**Tupperware party** pp. 167-169

Food votes
pp. 193-194

Sports fans
pp. 195-203

Authority
Chap. 6, pp. 208-236

Electric shock
pp. 208-215

Ear drops R ear
pp. 218-220

Tall PhD
pp. 222-223

Phone prescription
pp. 224-225

Parking meter
pp. 226-227

Bank scam
pp. 227-228

Honk!
p. 229

Scarcity (scar city)
Chap. 7, pp. 237-271

Plexiglass between toy
pp. 246-247

Romeo Romeo
pp. 248-249

Phosphate detergents
pp. 250-251

Insurance claims
pp. 254-255

Cookies
pp. 256-257

Soviet Union
pp. 259-260

Poseidon Adventure
pp. 264-265

3

Mnemonic Graphics for the Book *Cracking Creativity*

In *Cracking Creativity*, Michael Michalko exposes the thought processes used by creativity superstars. Leonardo DaVinci, Edison, Galileo, Mozart, and Einstein all had the ability to look at the same thing as everyone else but see something different. There are numerous examples of creativity at work, such as the consultant who transformed the transport industry by suggesting container ships, or the dog walker who saw annoying burrs on his dog's fur as Velcro, or the scientist who used a rejected adhesive to create Post-It notes. Just as a craftsperson has hand tools, a creative person has unique thinking tools. Memorizing this book will install a readily accessible set of creativity tools in your brain.

Explanation of Graphic Construction

Concepts in the book *Cracking Creativity* were transformed into 114 metaphorical illustrations—graphic substitutions. Below each illustration is a gray box (figure 3-1). It contains a short description of what the graphic refers to in the book. In addition to these descriptor words, you will occasionally find parentheses around several words. This parenthetical group of words is an explanation of how the substitute image was derived. In this example, the closest sounding wording to "Metaphor" is "metal four." There are only a few of these. Most graphics make sense after reading the appropriate section in *Cracking Creativity*. The page numbers for the specific section of the book referenced by the graphic are listed at the end of the description and are based on the 1998 edition of *Cracking Creativity* (ISBN 0-89815-913-X) published by Ten Speed Press.

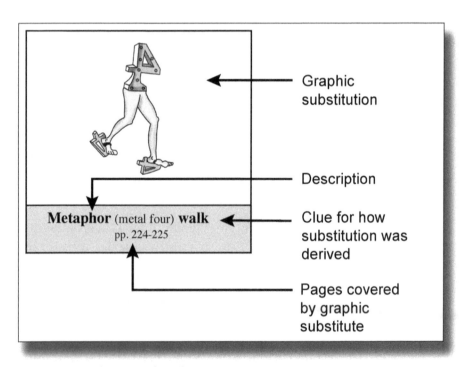

3-1 Explanation of graphic construction.

Part I: Seeing what no one else sees pp. 8-9, 15-80	**Strategy 1: Knowing how to see** p. 19
Flanged tracks vs. flanged wheels p. 20	**Invitational stem** p. 20
Global/specific abstractions pp. 23-27	**Container cargo ships** pp. 24-25

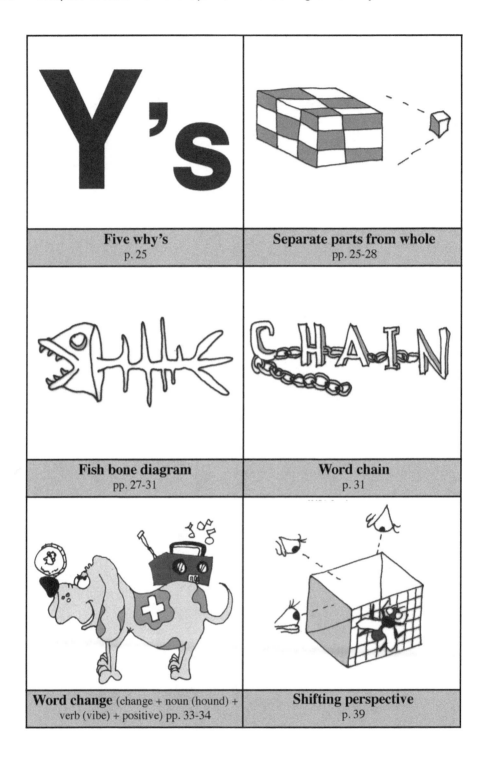

Five why's p. 25	Separate parts from whole pp. 25-28
Fish bone diagram pp. 27-31	Word chain p. 31
Word change (change + noun (hound) + verb (vibe) + positive) pp. 33-34	Shifting perspective p. 39

Gender change
pp. 40-41

Take on a different role
pp. 44-45

Child-like colored questions
pp. 47-49

Strategy 2: Visible thought—Galileo
pp. 9, 24, 51

Mind-mapping
pp. 55-65

Lotus diagram
pp. 66-68

Force field analysis pp. 75-78	**Visual brainstorming** pp. 79-80
Part II: Thinking what no one else is thinking pp. 81-281	**3 cuts, 8 pieces** p. 82
Strategy 3: Think fluently—immense productivity pp. 85-111	**Edison productive patents** p. 85

Defer judgment p. 86	**Pearl diving: idea quota** (quotes) pp. 89-92
List ideas pp. 92-93	**S.c.a.m.p.e.r.: Substitution** pp. 95-97
s.C.a.m.p.e.r.: Combine pp. 95, 97	**s.c.A.m.p.e.r.: Adapt** (chameleons adapt) pp. 95, 97

s.c.a.**M**.p.e.r.: **Magnify**
pp. 95, 97-98

s.c.a.m.**P**.e.r.: **Put to another use**
pp. 95, 98-99

s.c.a.m.p.**E**.r.: **Eliminate**
pp. 95, 99

s.c.a.m.p.e.**R**.: **Reverse**
pp. 95, 99

Take it apart: Toaster
pp. 100-101

Take it apart: Fasten the candle
p. 102

Edison's notebooks
pp. 105-107

Strategy 4: Novel combinations
pp. 113-138

DaVinci's grotesque heads
pp. 115-117

Combining the unrelated
p. 128

Combine domains
p. 138

Strategy 5: Connect the unconnected
pp. 139-172

DaVinci's sponge
p. 140

DaVinci's sound and water
p. 140

Random words
pp. 144-154

List characteristics
pp. 145-146

Force connections
p. 146

What's the essence?
pp. 146-147

Create many connections
pp. 147-148

Random objects
pp. 154-158

Thought walk
pp. 155-156

Removing ice from power lines
p. 156

Newspapers and magazines
pp. 157-158

Heavy generator, no crane
pp. 157-158

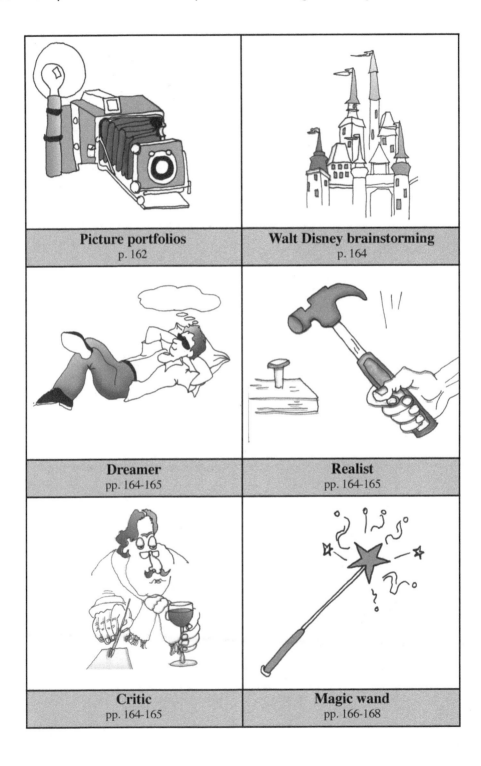

Picture portfolios
p. 162

Walt Disney brainstorming
p. 164

Dreamer
pp. 164-165

Realist
pp. 164-165

Critic
pp. 164-165

Magic wand
pp. 166-168

Tasty fish keep moving p. 168	**Paper airplane** pp. 168-170
Change relationship words pp. 170-172	**Strategy 6: Look at other side** pp. 173-193
Reversals pp. 174-176	**Lines** p. 175

Reversing Ass-sumptions
pp. 177-179

Reverse perspective
pp. 180-182

Janusian thinking: seeing all sides
pp. 183-185

Dry ice sandblasting
p. 184

Paradox of the Pringles
pp. 186-187

Working backwards
pp. 187-188

Strategy 7: Looking in other worlds
pp. 195-225

TV furrows
p. 196

Parallel worlds
pp. 196-203

World of essences
pp. 203-206

World of special interests
pp. 206-207

World of nature
pp. 207-208

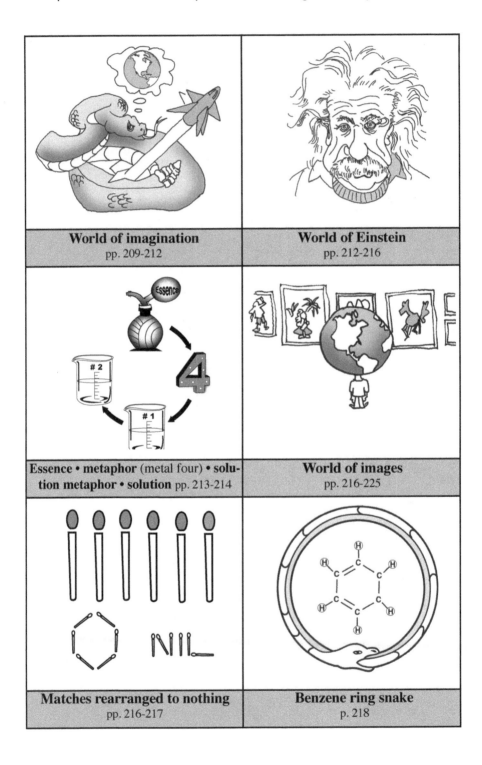

World of imagination
pp. 209-212

World of Einstein
pp. 212-216

Essence • metaphor (metal four) **• solution metaphor • solution** pp. 213-214

World of images
pp. 216-225

Matches rearranged to nothing
pp. 216-217

Benzene ring snake
p. 218

Pattern language pp. 218-220	**Sand tray** pp. 220-221
Creative collage pp. 222-224	**Metaphor** (metal four) **walk** pp. 224-225
Photo walk p. 225	**Strategy 8: Finding what not looking for—petri plate, fry pan** pp. 227-253

Plus, minus, interesting pp. 231-233	Latent potential (La tent): **Walkman, Post-it, Jacuzzi** pp. 234-237
Don't think about it pp. 238-239	Abstract definition pp. 239-241
Crazy ideas: Conductors, groups pp. 241-246	Opportunity headlines p. 252

Strategy 9: Collaborative-koinonia
(coin on knee) pp. 255-281

Participant variety and equality
p. 258

Suspend(ers) **Ass-umptions**
pp. 259-260

Suspend judgment
p. 260

Environment
pp. 260-261

Playfulness
p. 261

Facilitator	Stating the problem
pp. 261-262	p. 262
Idea production	Elaboration (bells and whistles)
pp. 262-263	p. 263
Clarifying questions	Recording
pp. 263-264	p. 264

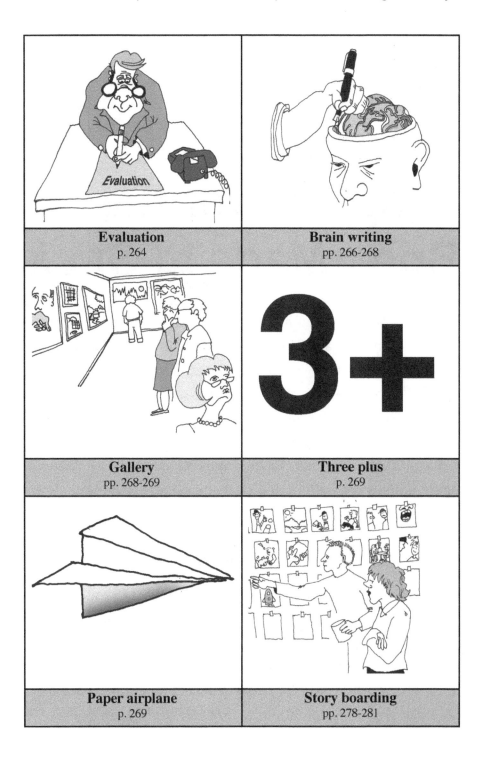

Evaluation p. 264	**Brain writing** pp. 266-268
Gallery pp. 268-269	**Three plus** p. 269
Paper airplane p. 269	**Story boarding** pp. 278-281

4

Mnemonic Graphics for the Book *Made to Stick*

In *Made to Stick*, the Heath brothers provide a formula for making your communication interesting, memorable, and potentially life changing. Stories of Texan litter bugs, waking up in a bathtub filled with ice cubes, the rings of Saturn, and crashing mini-vans illustrate six principles for making ideas stick in people's brains. They provide an acronymic formula, SUCCESs (the small "s" is not a typo), that can help teachers, parents, employers, entrepreneurs, employees, writers, and students make their communication more "sticky."

Explanation of Graphic Construction

Concepts in the book *Made to Stick* were transformed into 76 metaphorical illustrations—graphic substitutions. Below each illustration is a gray box (figure 4-1). It contains a short description of what the graphic refers to in the book. In addition to these descriptor words, you will occasionally find parentheses around several words. This parenthetical group of words is an explanation of how the substitute image was derived. In this example, the closest sounding wording to "Template" is "temple plate." There are only a few of these. Most graphics make sense after reading the appropriate section in *Made to Stick*. The page numbers for the specific section of the book referenced by the graphic are listed at the end of the description and are based on the 2007 edition of *Made to Stick* (ISBN 978-1-4000-6428-1) published by Random House.

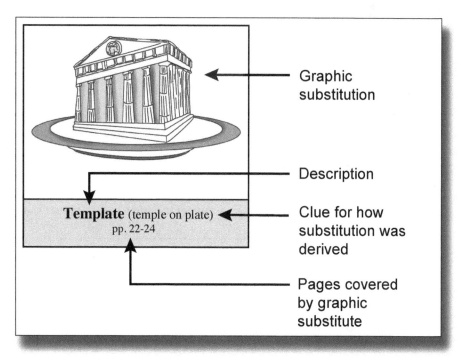

4-1 Explanation of graphic construction.

Kidney heist pp. 3-5	**Fat popcorn** pp. 6-8
Halloween candy pp. 13-14	**Success** (simple, unexpected, concrete, credible, emotional, story) pp. 16-19
Tap tune: Curse of knowledge pp. 19-20	**Template** (temple on plate) pp. 22-24

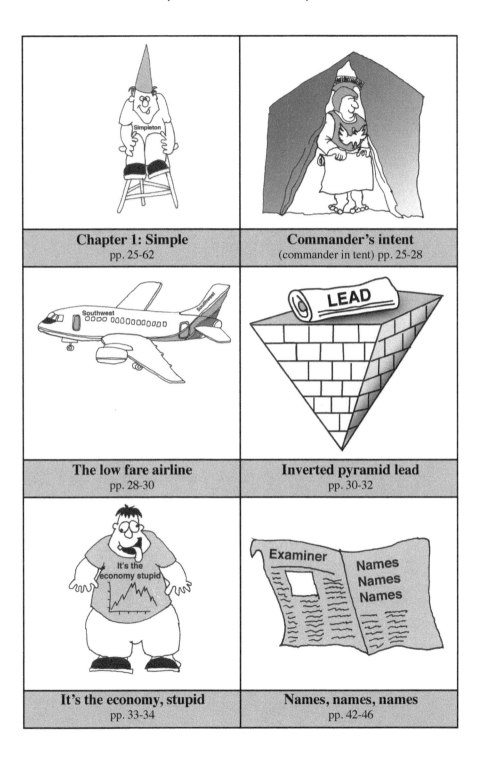

Chapter 1: Simple
pp. 25-62

Commander's intent
(commander in tent) pp. 25-28

The low fare airline
pp. 28-30

Inverted pyramid lead
pp. 30-32

It's the economy, stupid
pp. 33-34

Names, names, names
pp. 42-46

Simple, core, compact pp. 47-48	**A bird in the hand** pp. 47-48
Visual proverb: Palm Pilot pp. 48-50	**One vs. three bits information** pp. 51-52
Schema (ski ma) **pomelo** pp. 53-55	**High concept pitch** (Alien=jaws on a spaceship) pp. 57-59

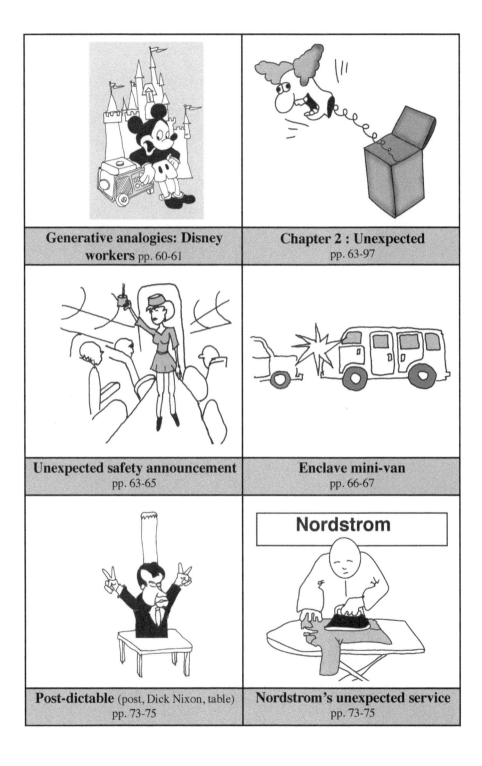

Generative analogies: Disney workers pp. 60-61	**Chapter 2 : Unexpected** pp. 63-97
Unexpected safety announcement pp. 63-65	**Enclave mini-van** pp. 66-67
Post-dictable (post, Dick Nixon, table) pp. 73-75	**Nordstrom's unexpected service** pp. 73-75

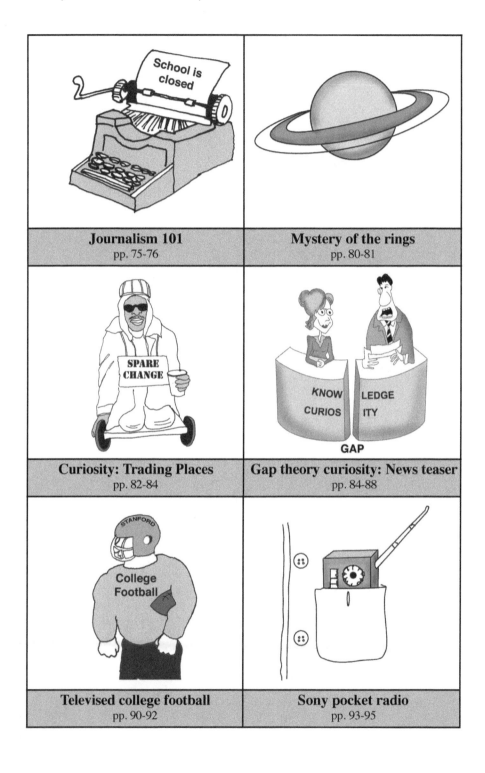

Journalism 101 pp. 75-76	Mystery of the rings pp. 80-81
Curiosity: Trading Places pp. 82-84	Gap theory curiosity: News teaser pp. 84-88
Televised college football pp. 90-92	Sony pocket radio pp. 93-95

Kennedy's man on moon pp. 96-97	**Chapter 3: Concrete** pp. 98-129
Aesop's sour grapes pp. 98-100	**Nature Conservancy: Mt. Hamilton** pp. 100-104
Concrete Asian math pp. 104-106	**Velcro theory math** pp. 109-111

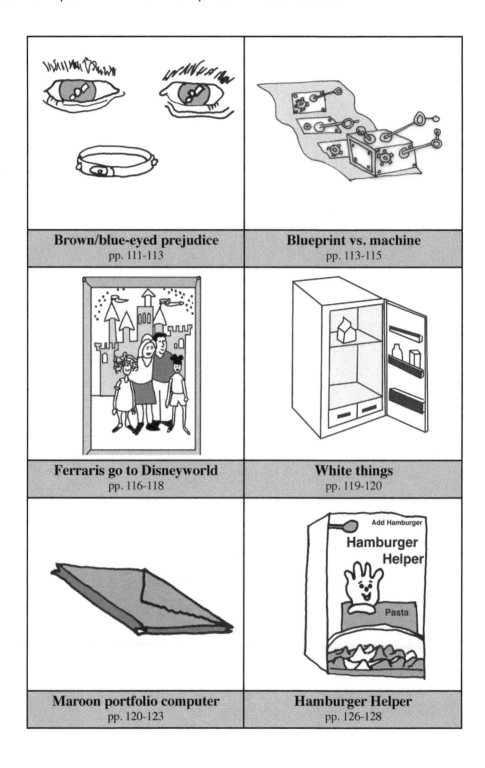

Brown/blue-eyed prejudice pp. 111-113	Blueprint vs. machine pp. 113-115
Ferraris go to Disneyworld pp. 116-118	White things pp. 119-120
Maroon portfolio computer pp. 120-123	Hamburger Helper pp. 126-128

Saddleback Sam's church pp. 128-129	**Chapter 4: Credible** (credit card) pp. 130-164
Ulcer bacteria pp. 130-132	**Anti-authority: Smoking cancer patient** pp. 135-136
Details (the tails) pp. 137-138	**Darth Vader toothbrush detail** pp. 138-139

Nuclear bucket BBs pp. 141-143	**Sinatra test: Harry Potter India** pp. 151-152
Edible fabric dye plant pp. 153-155	**Falsifiable claim Wendy's** pp. 155-157
Rookie orientation AIDS pp. 162-163	**Chapter 5: Emotion** pp. 165-203

Save the Children
pp. 165-167

Tobacco ads
pp. 169-171

Semantic stretch (seaman tick):
Unique pp. 171-174

Sportsmanship: Honor the game
pp. 174-177

They laughed until I played
pp. 177-180

Cable TV promo
pp. 180-182

Maslow's pyramid pp. 182-185	**Pegasus chow hall Iraq** pp. 186-187
Fireman's popcorn popper gift pp. 187-188	**Don't mess with Texas: Litter** pp. 195-199
Duo Pianos: Three Why's pp. 199-201	**ER simulation** pp. 201-202

Chapter 6: Story pp. 204-237	**Neonatal nurse** pp. 204-206
Xerox repair stories pp. 206-208	**Mental simulation** p. 213
Jarred's Subway weight loss pp. 218-224	**Challenge plot: David & Goliath** pp. 226-227

Connection plot: Good Samaritan pp. 227-229

Creativity plot: Ingersoll Rand grinder pp. 229-231

World Bank: Springboard stories pp. 231-235

Curse of knowledge: Stanford speakers pp. 242-245

5

Tips and Tricks for Memorizing Books

This chapter contains tips to help you memorize books or parts of books. Let's start with how your memory works.

Making Memories

Imagine that the part of your brain responsible for making memories is a little old man. He's reading a book (figure 5-1). The book represents the distractions of life, those unfettered thoughts that dance through your mind like jitterbugging monkeys: "Is it lunch time yet?" "What is a hornless unicorn?," "Did I leave the stove on?," "Can a trout drown?," "Would *Victoria's Secret* be as popular if it were *Broomhilda's Secret*?" ...

5-1 Imagine that the part of your brain responsible for making memories is a little old man reading a book. The book represents the distractions of life.

If you want your little old man to learn something new, he needs to put down the distracting book and concentrate (figure 5-2). To memorize the picture chains presented in this book, you need to focus on one picture at a time. Our conscious brain is not designed to multi-task. If you disagree, find the seventh letter in the alphabet starting from A while simultaneously finding the seventh letter starting from Z. You can rapidly switch back and forth between the two tasks, but your brain can process only one at a time.

5-2 To make a memory, you have to ignore distractions and pay attention to the information you want to memorize. Our little old man puts down his distracting book.

Now that we have our little old man's attention, we are going to have him memorize an image. We have a choice of two types of memory—short term and long term. Short-term memories are measured in seconds. The name someone told you at a party and you promptly forgot, the chore your spouse asked you to do which went into your memory trash bin and you forgot to take out the real trash, the page you just read but don't remember, or that brilliant idea you had while driving to work that vanished in the traffic. This is your short-term memory.

Long-term memory is what memorizing books is all about. Examples of long-term memories are your birth date, social security number, combination to your gym locker, and directions to your home.

Scientists have discovered one secret for making long-term memories. It involves forming protein in your brain. If you don't make protein, the information disappears.[18, 19, 20, 21, 22, 23] So our little old man gets up from his comfy chair to prepare some protein. To prepare the protein, imagine him frying an egg (a protein) (figure 5-3).

5-3 To make a long-term memory, you have to start by making protein. This is represented by the little old man frying an egg.

He fries the egg but he does it very quickly. As he lifts the pan to see if it sticks, it slides off (figure 5-4). The memory didn't stick.

5-4 If our little old man fries the egg too quickly, it doesn't stick to
the pan. If you don't concentrate on what you want long enough,
it won't make a long-term memory.

What went wrong? The problem is that you have to pay
attention for 10 or more uninterrupted seconds. No picking the
book up. If you are trying to fix an image in your mind, you need
to keep it on your mental screen for at least 10 seconds. Think of
this as the 10-second rule. The little old man concentrates on frying his egg for 10 seconds (figure 5-5).

5-5 It takes time to make the protein that creates a long-term memory. The little old man cooks his protein for 10 seconds.

The protein has enough time to cook. Now it sticks to the pan making a long-term memory (figure 5-6).

5-6 Given enough time to form protein, brains make long-term memories. The egg sticks to the pan.

When you imagine the substitution pictures and the action linking one picture to the next picture in the chain, retain the image for a minimum of 10 seconds. Give the little old man inside your brain enough time to cook the protein. This 10-second rule helps make long-term memories.

When to Practice

If you are as busy as a bee, beaver, or multi-tasking-PhD-triath-lete-entrepreneur-charity organizing-chauffeuring-single-soccer mom/dad, here are some unusual times to practice chaining your images together.

Exercising: When you go for a walk, take along a copy of the graphic substitutions for the book you are memorizing. Memorize the first six illustrations and link them into a chain. As you walk, walk through the chain in your mind. When you feel comfortable, add six more images to your chain until you have the whole sequence down. Then go for another walk and mentally walk through the entire chain. As you arrive at each picture in the chain, make sure you can explain what it means. If you have trouble explaining a graphic, go back to the book and read that section again (use the page numbers listed under each graphic in Chapters 2, 3, and 4). You can also practice your chain while:

- Running
- Swimming (use a lap counter to keep track of your laps, so your mind is free to visualize)
- Biking
- Weight lifting (decide how many images it takes to reach a count of 6, 12, 18 reps. Then rather than count-

ing your reps, imagine each image until you reach the rep number you want. Build your muscles and your mind.)

Exercise will also help improve your memory. Aerobic exercise has been shown to increase the size of the hippocampus which is implicated in long-term memory storage.[24, 25, 26, 27]

Dead time: Turn "waiting time" into a memory work out:

- Caught in crawl traffic, turn road boredom into memory muscle. Don't do this when driving at normal speeds as you can zone into the chain and forget about your main task, driving.
- Airport waiting area (especially when standing in your socks waiting to go through the scanner)
- Plane flights
- Bus stops
- Bus rides
- Boring meetings
- Showering
- Waiting for your waiter
- Breakfast, lunch, dinner instead of the newspaper
- Post office lines
- Grocery store check out line
- Solitary confinement at San Quentin

Sleeping: Before retiring, chain six pictures and their meanings. Memory consolidation during sleep may actually aid the memory process.[28, 29, 30, 31, 32] In the morning, see if you can recall the chain. Every night, add another six images until you have completed the chain.

Games: Turn your memory chain into a game. You can play with friends, children, spouses, anyone who wants to memorize the same book you have chosen. Start by describing the first picture in the chain and what it represents. Then your partner describes and explains the next picture in the chain. Keep alternating until you finish the book. Think of it as a memory book club.

Act it out: In memory workshops, I ask students to partner up. One student takes on the role of the director of a play. The other student is the actor. Then the action begins. The director describes the first scene in a memory chain and her partner, like Charlie Chaplin, silently acts out the scene. Like acts in a play, the director prompts the actor from one scene to the next. When the team makes it through a chain, they switch roles. This mini-acting class enhances the memory of the chain. Both students started out by memorizing the chained script on a visual level. When they work through the roles of director and actor, it adds a verbal and physical component that strengthens the memory. Research on rats suggests that memories are not stored in a single locus in the brain, but in multiple areas.[33] By including all three brain input sources—visual, auditory, and kinesthetic—memories are enhanced.

Apply Your Memory Techniques to Any Book

Choosing a book to memorize is like choosing a friend—pick a good one. Three questions can help you decide which books to memorize:

1. Ask people you admire, "What are the three most life-changing books you've ever read?" Maybe they'll men-

tion the book *Learned Optimism* by Martin Seligman. If the book sounds interesting, leaf through it. If you think it contains valuable information, memorize it.

2. Ask yourself, "Will the ideas in this book help me become the person I want to be?" Maybe adding humor to your life by memorizing Judy Carter's *Stand-Up Comedy: The Book* will give you tools to make people laugh.

3. Ask yourself, "Will having ready access to the ideas in this book help me?" If you choose a book like *Drawing on the Right Side of the Brain* by Betty Edwards, you have an outline of how to teach yourself and someone else to draw. As an art instructor, you could pull it up at any time. If you are a biologist, geologist, electrician, beautician, salesperson, tree surgeon, or witch—what book contains information that would help you if it was in your mind all the time?

Steps to Commit Any Book to Memory

1. Read the book and highlight the main points.
2. Create substitute images for highlighted concepts.
3. Sketch your images in the margin of the book next to the highlighted point it pertains to.
4. Chain images together in your mind.

Highlight main points: When choosing a book to memorize, make it an easy one—one in which the author uses stories, pictures, graphics, and metaphors to make important points. This type of book is easier to visualize than one with abstract material. Highlight significant points with a marker.

Create images: At the completion of each chapter, review the highlighted points. At the first point, ask yourself, what's the most outstanding feature about this point? Take that outstanding feature and create an image. To create memorable images, make them outrageous and filled with action!

Sketch your graphic metaphor: In the margin of the book you are memorizing, opposite each highlighted section, make a simple sketch of your graphic metaphor. When you check back later, especially if the book has a lot of chapters, these sketches will refresh your memory.

Chain images together: After creating an image for each important point in a chapter, you're ready for the next step. Starting at the beginning, link the images together. This linkage acts as a transition between images. Like boxcars in a train, each image is coupled to the next by an action. When chaining, put action into the transitions.

Practice: As you add images, periodically run through the chain. Be sure you remember what each image represents. Chains can be practiced anytime and anywhere.

If your chain is long or complex, links may fade with time. If this happens, refresh your memory by referring back to the sketches you made in the margins of the book. If you want to solidify your book memory, practice at periodic intervals. Check your memory after a week, a month, and a year.

Notes and Sources

1   Verghese, Joe, Richard B. Lipton, et al. Leisure activities and the risk of dementia in the elderly. *The New England Journal of Medicine*, 348: (2003): 2508–2516.

2   Hall, C.B., R.B. Lipton, et al. Cognitive activities delay onset of memory decline in persons who develop dementia. *Neurology*, 73 (5) August 4, 2009: 356–361.

3   Small, Gary, Gigi Vorgan. *The Alzheimer's Prevention Program: Keep Your Brain Healthy for the Rest of Your Life*. New York: Workman Publishing, 2011.

4   Pillai, Jagan, Charles B. Hall, et al. Association of crossword puzzle participation with memory decline in persons who develop dementia. *Journal of the International Neuropsychological Society*, (6) November 17, 2011: 1006–1013.

5   Worland, Justin. Can Brain Games Keep My Mind Young? *Time*, February 2015, vol. 185, no. 6–7. Refers to an open letter put out by the Stanford Center on Longevity and endorsed by 70 prominent brain scientists and psychologists critical of the benefits of Internet games purported to enhance the brain's cognitive processing ability.

6   Bramly, Serge. *Leonardo: Discovering the Life of Leonardo da Vinci*. New York: Harper, 1991: 257–258.

7   The Leader-in-Training program is an intensive leadership program taught to teens ages 15–17 each year at Deer Crossing Camp, www.deercrossingcamp.com.

8   Wiltens, Jim. *Memory Smart: Nine memory skills every grade schooler needs*. Redwood City: Deer Crossing Press, 2003, 95–106. Chapter 9 includes a short booklet of facts about African animals. As an aid in memorizing the details in this booklet, the facts are converted into metaphorical images. The images are subsequently chained together. Memorizing this chain enables the reader to recall the facts.

9   Gehring, Robert E., Michael P. Toglia, Gregory A. Kimble. Recognition memory for words and pictures at short and long retention intervals. *Memory and Cognition,* Vol. 4 (3) (1976): 256–260.

10   Stenberg, Georg. Conceptual and perceptual factors in the picture superiority effect. *European Journal of Cognitive Psychology,* (2006): 1–35.

11   Hockley, William E. The picture superiority effect in associative recognition. *Memory and Cognition,* 36 (7) (2008): 1351–1359.

12   Brady, Timothy F., Talia Konkle, et al. Visual long-term memory has a massive storage capacity for object details. *Proceedings National Academy Sciences* 105, no. 38 (2008): 14325–14329. Participants were shown 2,500 pictures over 5.5 hours. Afterwards they were shown pairs of images and asked to indicate which they had seen. Accuracy was in the range of 87–92%.

13   Yates, Frances A. *The Art of Memory*. Chicago: University of Chicago Press, 1966.

14   Carruthers, Mary, and Jan M. Ziolkowski, eds. *The Medieval Craft of Memory: An anthology of texts and pictures*. Philadelphia: University of Pennsylvania Press, 2004.

15   Rupp, Rebecca. *Committed to Memory: How we remember*

and why we forget. New York: Crown Publishers, 1998: 282. To memorize a speech, Mark Twain would convert the concepts of his speech into graphic metaphors—images. He would then go to a park and mentally place the images on landmarks in the park such as a park bench, civil war monument, and on top of a band stand. To remember the order of points in his speech, he would take a mental walk through the park. At each landmark, he would remember the image he had placed there which in turn reminded him of the next point in his speech.

16   Foer, Joshua. *Moonwalking with Einstein: The art and science of remembering everything.* New York: The Penguin Press, 2011: 121. You can experience the rapid foreign language acquisition described here by playing the card game *SNAP! Spanish Nouns: Deck 1* by Jim Wiltens. The card game uses the mnemonic technique of substitution to learn 48 Spanish nouns in minutes.

17   A rotated D with a J underneath looks like an umbrella.

18   Barondes, Samuel H. Cerebral protein synthesis inhibitors block long term memory. *International Review of Neurobiology,* 12 (1970): 177–205.

19   Pedreira, Eugenia M., Beatriz Dimant, Héctor Maldonado. Inhibitors of protein and RNA synthesis block context memory and long-term habituation in the crab *Chasmagnathus. Pharmacology, Biochemistry and Behavior*, vol 54, issue 3, July 1996: 611–617.

20   Rupp, Rebecca. *Committed to Memory: How we remember and why we forget.* New York: Crown Publishers, 1998: 128–130. Rats, goldfish, praying mantises, and chicks stop learning when injected with protein inhibitors.

21   Fields, Douglas R. Making memories stick. *Scientific American Magazine*, February 2005: 74–81.

22   Kandel, Eric R. *In Search of Memory: The emergence of a new science of mind.* New York: W. W. Norton and Company Inc., 2006: 212–215. A Nobel prize winner, Kandel did research on the lowly sea slug. A sea slug has 20,000 brain cells. Mammals have up to 100 billion. This makes it easier to work on a slug. Memory tests showed that long-term memories in the slug were disrupted by drugs that prevent protein formation. Highly recommended if you are interested in the science of memory.

23   Sutton, Michael A., Erin M. Schuman. Dendritic protein synthesis, synaptic plasticity, and memory. *Cell,* Vol 127 (1), October 6, 2006: 49–58.

24   Ratey, John J., Eric Hagerman. *Spark: The revolutionary new science of exercise and the brain.* New York: Little Brown and Company, 2008: 35–56. A good overview of the benefits of exercise on the brain. For example, students learn vocabulary words 20% faster following exercise. This exercise is correlated with a rise in brain-derived neurotrophic factor (BDNF). Think of BDNF as fertilizer for the brain. It encourages growth (plasticity).

25   Hillman, Charles H., Kirk I. Erickson, Arthur F. Kramer. Be smart, exercise your heart: Exercise effects on brain and cognition. *Nature Reviews Neuroscience* 9, January 2008: 58–65.

26   Erickson, Kirk I., Michelle W. Voss, et al. Exercise training increases size of hippocampus and improves memory. *Proceedings of the National Academy of Sciences of the United States of America,* Vol. 108, no. 7, February 15, 2011: 3017–3022.

27   Chapman, Sandra B., Sina Aslan, et al. Shorter term aerobic exercise improves brain, cognition, and cardiovascular fitness in aging. *Frontiers in Aging Neuroscience,* vol. 5, article 75, November 2013: 1–9.

28   Drosopoulos, Spyridon, Wagner Ulrich, Jan Born. Sleep Enhances Explicit Recollection in Recognition Memory. *Learning Memory*, 12 (1) January 2005: 44–51.

29   Hill, Catherine M., Alexandra M. Hogan, Annette Karmiloff-Smith. To Sleep, perchance to enrich learning? *Archives of Disease in Childhood,* 92 (2007): 637–643.

30   Diekelmann, Susanne. The memory function of sleep. *Nature Reviews Neuroscience* 11, February 2010: 114–126.

31   Prince, Toni-Moi, Ted Abel. The Impact of Sleep Loss on Hippocampal Function. *Learning Memory,* (20) October 2013: 558–569.

32   Lewis, Penelope. *The Secret World of Sleep: The surprising science of the mind at rest.* New York: Palgrave Macmillan, 2013. An overview of how sleep affects memory.

33   Searleman, Alan, Hermann Douglas. *Memory from a Broader Perspective.* New York: McGraw-Hill, 1994: 146–147. Researchers trained rats to run a maze for a reward. After a rat had memorized the maze (demonstrated by rapidly running the maze and not going to dead ends), a part of the rat's brain was destroyed. The researchers were attempting to localize that portion of the brain that had the "maze memory." The experiment did not work. While the damaged rats were not as quick, they still ran the maze faster than their first attempts when they were learning the maze.

Index

About the Author

Jim Wiltens has worked with corporate clients such as Stanford University and Google as well as consulted with many school districts on the topics of Memory, Leadership, and Creativity. He has authored six books including *Memory Smart*. One of his projects was the development of *SNAP!*, a memory game that teaches a foreign language. He is director/owner of Deer Crossing Camp, a summer camp designed to bring out the best qualities in children (www.deercrossingcamp.com). His initial interest in mnemonics came when students in the leadership training programs at Deer Crossing Camp asked if there was a better way than rote repetition to retain all the information they were learning. That's when he started researching mnemonics and looking for practical ways of introducing these powerful memory techniques to his leadership candidates.

Jim has also been an award-winning columnist, research marine biologist, chemist, university coach of championship teams, and professional adventurer. On one adventure, he used his memory techniques to learn Mongolian so that he could communicate with the people he encountered as he rode camels across the Gobi Desert in search of the cousin of a Tyrannosaurus Rex. To find out more about Jim's programs and workshops:

www.jimwiltens.com

jim@jimwiltens.com